REAL WORLD ECONOMICS™

How the
Stock Market
Works

Kathy Furgang

+6.73
+1.33
+21.64
+14.83
+9.19
+3.24
+32.47
+11.02
+2.35
+0.21
+25.05
+2.42
+5.53
+12.41

ROSEN
PUBLISHING®

New York

To Dad

Published in 2011 by The Rosen Publishing Group, Inc.
29 East 21st Street, New York, NY 10010

Library of Congress Cataloging-in-Publication Data

Furgang, Kathy.
How the stock market works / Kathy Furgang.
    p. cm.—(Real world economics)
Includes bibliographical references and index.
ISBN 978-1-4358-9466-2 (library binding)
1. Stock exchanges—Juvenile literature. 2. Stocks—Juvenile literature.
I. Title.
HG4553.F87 2011
332.64'2—dc22

2009045687

Manufactured in the United States of America

CPSIA Compliance Information: Batch #S10YA: For further information, contact Rosen Publishing, New York, New York, at 1-800-237-9932.

On the cover: The U.S. stock market affects financial markets all around the world.

Contents

INTRODUCTION

It's hard to turn on the television or look at a newspaper without seeing news about the stock market. One often hears reports that the stock market was up or down today. The meaning of these reports is sometimes difficult for people to understand. They may think that the stock market does not affect them. But it does indeed affect our everyday lives. The stock market affects nearly everything we do. Primarily, it has a strong effect on our economy, which is the overall wealth of a region or country.

So what is the stock market? And how does it work? One of the most important things that people should know is that the stock market is not a bank. When you put money in a bank, it is almost always safe. The bank will give the money back to a depositor whenever he or she is ready to use it. That is not the case with the stock market. People who put their money in the stock market can lose it all if the stocks that they

invest in go down, or lose value. They can also make more—sometimes much more—than they invested if their stocks go up, or increase in value.

The stock market can be risky. So if the stock market is a risk, why do people invest in it? The reason is that it offers many opportunities for people to make a lot of money. These opportunities are what have kept the stock market a vital engine for the economy and American business and industry for more than a century.

CHAPTER ONE

What Is the Stock Market?

We have all seen the following chaotic scene on TV or in the movies: People dressed in suits rush across a crowded floor, chatter on phones, and yell back and forth to each other as they wave little pieces of paper in the air. All the while, they glance up at numbers that flash on computer screens and electronic scrolls that surround them. This scene depicts the stock market at work. The people you see running around are working at a stock exchange. They are helping people all around the world buy and sell stocks, which are ownership shares of companies.

A stock market is a place that sells stocks. A stock is a partial ownership of a company. These partial ownerships are also called shares. When someone owns one or more shares of a company, he or she is known as a shareholder. This person becomes part owner of that company. Anyone who puts his or her money into the stock market by buying shares of companies is called an investor. An investor hopes to make a profit

Stockbrokers on Wall Street work in a fast-paced, hectic environment.

with his or her investment. There are many opportunities to make money in the stock market. If a company does well, its profits go up and shareholders make money. However, if a company does not do well and its profits slow or decrease, a shareholder may lose money.

The people who run around the stock exchange floor are called stockbrokers. They work all day to help people buy or sell shares of companies. Suppose a company is selling its shares for $10 each. An investor might want to buy ten shares. So he or she pays $100 and then owns a very small portion of the company. The investor may make more money than he or she spent on the stock purchase if the company does well and makes a profit. A company that sells shares of its company to the public is called a public company. Companies "go public" and sell stock in order to raise more money to operate—to hire more employees, to expand operations, and to research and develop new products.

Wall Street

The financial center of the U.S. economy is located at the southern tip of the island of Manhattan on a narrow laneway called Wall Street. This is the site of the New York Stock Exchange (NYSE). In this building is where most stock buying and selling is done in the United States. This constant buying and selling of stocks is called trading.

The history of Wall Street goes back almost four hundred years, long before there was even a nation known as the United States. Dutch explorers and colonists settled Manhattan back in 1625. (*Manhatta* is a Lenape word meaning "island of many hills.") They called the place New Amsterdam. It was part of New Netherland, a Dutch colony stretching from Cape Cod in the north to the Delmarva Peninsula in the south. In 1653, the Dutch built a 12-foot (3.66 m) wooden wall in lower Manhattan that spanned from the East River to the Hudson River. The wall was intended as protection against Native Americans as well as the British. In 1685, after the wall was torn down, Wall Street was built running parallel to where the defensive wall originally stood.

From the beginning, Wall Street was a central meeting place for merchants who wished to trade commodities. Commodities

In 1685, Wall Street was built in Manhattan. Today, it is home to the New York Stock Exchange and is considered the financial capital of the United States and the world.

are goods that have not been processed yet, such as wheat, tobacco, or cotton. Even slaves just arrived from Africa on slave ships were traded on Wall Street, which was near the city's port and large harbor.

Almost a century later, after Britain had seized control of Manhattan and the entire New York Colony from the Dutch, the thirteen colonies began to chafe under British rule. Rebellions began to break out, and lower Manhattan was a common place for protest. During the Revolutionary War, hundreds of houses along Wall Street were burned down, most likely by patriots who did not want to surrender the city to the British.

In 1792, following the Revolution, a group of twenty-four brokers decided to form a group devoted to the selling of public stocks. They would be paid by other people to trade stocks for them. The brokers signed an agreement under a buttonwood tree at 68 Wall Street and continued to do their work there for years, moving to a coffee house in the winter. The document they signed, known as the Buttonwood Agreement, formed the first formal New York stock exchange. In 1817, the organization created a constitution and was officially renamed the New York Stock and Exchange Board. Today, this organization is simply known as

In 1792, the New York Stock Exchange Board first met outside 68 Wall Street under a buttonwood tree.

the New York Stock Exchange. That same year, operations moved to a rented room ($200/month) at 40 Wall Street.

Brokers had to belong to the New York Stock Exchange in order to do business there. That did not stop outside brokers from earning money on their own, however. These outside brokers traded securities right on the street corners of Wall Street. Securities are certificates of stocks that prove a person's partial ownership in a company.

Communicating on Wall Street

Stockbrokers must be able to communicate prices to each other in order to buy and sell stocks. In the early 1800s, messengers raced back and forth between brokerage houses with hand-written orders to buy and sell stocks. Sharing information with stock exchanges in other cities was more difficult. Men used flags to signal the prices of stocks. People set up along an intercity route used telescopes to read, record, and pass on this information to the next person along the route. Both of these methods were replaced with Morse code once Samuel Morse invented the telegraph in 1838.

By 1867, the ticker tape machine was invented. This allowed all of the brokerage houses to get the same information at the same time along a long strip of paper called a ticker tape. A clerk would then write the stock prices on a board for everyone to see. Eventually, this method was replaced with electronic displays. Today, stock prices instantly flash on television, computer, and cell phone screens around the world. There are even huge scrolling electronic tickers in public places, like New York City's Times Square.

Capitalism

Can the public be part owners of companies in any area around the world? Do all countries sell and trade shares in their public companies? Most of them do, but not all. The system that allows the United States and many other countries to trade and sell goods and shares of companies is called capitalism. According to the ideas of capitalism, anyone has the right to manufacture and sell goods for a profit. American companies can make more money to help develop, run, and expand their businesses by getting public support in the form of cash investments. They might use the funds raised through sales of stocks to hire more workers, build new factories, develop new or improved products, or simply pocket the profits and get richer. A company that does not pass along some of the profits to its shareholders, however, or funnel profits back into business operations and development probably won't remain successful for long.

The stocks of companies that manufacture and sell products or services that are in high demand usually rise. More people are interested in these companies because they are developing popular products or services, selling a lot of units, and making a lot of money. Companies that do not have a successful product may find that their stock prices are dropping. People are not willing to take a risk and invest in that company if they don't feel their profits are rising and their products are good or desirable. The supply and demand of a company's stock often corresponds to that of the goods or services the company offers. If demand for a company's products is high, its stock tends to be in high demand, too. So the stock price rises. The opposite is true for a company whose products and services are not in high demand among consumers.

The goods we buy today are made for a global market. If they sell well, the stocks of the companies that make them will rise.

In today's markets, people buy and sell goods that are made in all areas of the world by American and foreign companies. This is called a global market. Investors may buy or sell stocks all around the world, too. Foreign investors can buy stock in

American companies, and American investors can purchase shares in publicly traded foreign businesses. The New York Stock Exchange is not the only one in the world. There are more than fifty major stock exchanges worldwide, on every continent except Antarctica.

Stock Indexes

Though not the only stock exchange, the New York Stock Exchange is the largest in the world in terms of market value. It is second largest in terms of the volume of transactions, behind the National Association of Securities Dealers Automated Quotations (NASDAQ). The NASDAQ is also based in New York. Each year, trillions of dollars of stock trade through the NYSE on four trading room floors. Brokers do the buying and selling at the direction of their customers, who place orders.

Several basic ways in which an investor can keep track of how the stock market is performing exist. There are three popular indexes that people can check to review stock results. They are the NASDAQ, the Dow Jones Industrial Average (often

Celebrities such as actress Sienna Miller can be seen visiting the New York Stock Exchange. Celebrities and dignitaries often ring the opening and closing bell of the NYSE.

referred to as "the Dow Jones" or "the Dow"), and the Standard and Poor's 500 (the S&P 500).

The NASDAQ, founded in 1971, is important for both brokers and investors. It is an electronic stock exchange where

brokers can buy and sell stocks via computer. About thirty-eight thousand companies trade their securities through this exchange. It has more trading volume per hour than any other exchange in the world.

The NASDAQ is an index as well as a stock exchange. A stock index is a measurement of the performance of a sample collection of companies' stocks, usually the stocks of the largest companies traded in that exchange. When the news reports that "the NASDAQ gained one hundred points today," that means the collective value of the stocks chosen for its index went up by that number of points. When the point value of the NASDAQ is reported, a percentage gain or loss is also reported. This is a more important indicator of how the stock market did that day. It may have gained 2 percent or lost 1.5 percent of its cumulative value (the total worth of the stock of the companies' in the index). These numbers let investors know if the stock market as a whole is gaining or losing value, since the companies in the index are taken to be representative of the larger economy.

17

Business news reports often state that "the Dow was up today" or "the Dow Jones took a hit today." The Dow Jones Industrial Average is another kind of index, or reference point, that gives an overall sense of how the stock market is doing. There is no way to quickly report the results of every company during the day, so the Dow is an average of the thirty most widely held and largest companies in the United States. The Dow does not indicate how every company that is traded on the NYSE performed. It is simply an average of some of the biggest of them.

The S&P 500 is another index for reporting stock averages. It is an index of five hundred companies, the largest ones holding a greater weight on the index than the smaller ones.

CHAPTER TWO
Riding the Highs and Lows of the Stock Market

The stock market, as well as the economy of the country and the world, goes through natural highs and lows. A period of good economic growth is called a period of prosperity. During these periods, it seems almost effortless for investors to make money on Wall Street. Companies are hiring a lot of workers. Salaries and job security are good. Money is flowing, and consumer confidence is high as a result. So the public is spending money on things they need and even on things they don't need. Companies are making large profits, which, in turn, results in even more hiring and higher salaries.

But economic upswings cannot continue forever. It is natural for the economy to slow down. A period in which the economy slows down is called a recession. During a recession, companies produce fewer goods, fewer employees are needed, and people are buying fewer goods. A recession can be a very trying period for all members of a society. The economy—and families—can be severely harmed when fewer people are employed and fewer consumers are buying goods in the market.

A recession can be a very trying period for all members of society. This man is attending a job fair, hoping to find work among the companies that are accepting résumés.

Vicious Cycle

Like throwing a stone into a pond, a recession can have a ripple effect on many other parts of the economy. When companies

need fewer workers, they must lay people off in order to continue to make a profit. At the same time, they are making fewer goods because consumer demand has gone down, in part because of insecurity over the economy. Laid-off workers will have less money to spend in their everyday lives because they no longer get a regular paycheck. They will not be able to buy new goods such as cars, TVs, clothing, and furniture. They will have less money to go to the movies, restaurants, and amusement parks.

The more companies that lay off people during a recession, the more people there are who cannot keep the economy running through consumer spending. Eventually, people who have been laid off may not be able to pay their rent or their mortgages. Even those workers who hang onto their jobs may be so worried about being laid off in the near future that they cut way back on their household spending and begin to save money instead.

What happens when fewer people are spending money in a slow economy? The economy slows even more. The companies

21

that let go of workers are now selling even fewer goods than before. So they make even smaller profits (or no profits at all) and may have to lay off even more workers. The companies' falling stock prices reflect their poor performance. As a result,

With fewer people able to shop for goods during a recession, stores may not be able to stay in business. This can weaken the economy even more and send stock prices still lower.

investors in these companies are no longer making any money. They may begin to lose confidence in the companies they have invested their money in. Investors may sell their stock, and those companies then have even less money to help them get

through the difficult times. Some companies can no longer make a profit and may fail altogether, declaring bankruptcy and going out of business.

The more businesses that slow down, the more people are affected throughout the economy at all income levels—rich, poor, and middle class. It can take months or even years, but the ripple effects of a recession can reach specific regions of the country, the nation at large, and even the world markets.

Burst Bubbles

What causes an economic slow-down in the first place? Many things can bring it about. But often it's the period of prosperity itself that indirectly causes an eventual slowdown. All of the companies that are involved in making the goods and services sold to consumers will be

23

doing great. If the companies are public, their stocks will likely be soaring and their investors will be happy that they are making money. The companies themselves will probably need to take on extra workers to keep up with the extra production needed to meet the increased demand for products and services. Hiring and salaries will probably increase. During a time when people have extra money to spend, they may decide to make "big ticket," or major, purchases like a new car or a vacation home.

But how many extra cars and homes can people buy? How long can company stocks soar as people buy these new products? The unusually high demand for a particular good or service is often called a bubble. But what happens to bubbles after a while? They burst. Like any other bubble, goods and services bubbles eventually burst. This means there suddenly won't be a great demand for the products that people bought in good economic times. The companies will need to produce fewer of these products. As a result, they will need to employ fewer workers. Unemployed workers or employees who fear unemployment will drastically cut their spending, resulting in still lower levels of product production, more layoffs, and even less consumer spending. This will cause a downward spiral throughout the economy that keeps worsening as time goes on.

Not all bubbles burst, however. Sometimes demand remains high, even if it slows a bit, and technological advancement and innovative product development can keep consumer appetites whetted. For example, during the first half of the twentieth century, there was a great demand for telephones. Families were just beginning to buy their first home phones. Previously, most telephones were in offices or public places like drug

Investing for Retirement

Not just rich investors put their money in the stock market. Many ordinary people invest money in accounts called mutual funds. A mutual fund collects funds from a pool of people and invests it in stocks, bonds, and securities. Hopefully, these pooled investments will see a good return (i.e., make money), and the earnings are then distributed among the fund's investors. These funds are managed and traded by professional brokers.

Many people use the stock market and mutual funds to help them save for their retirement. Companies often offer their employees 401(k) accounts. These accounts put money into many different public companies so that they can grow in value before the employee retires. Individuals can also buy such accounts, called individual retirement accounts, or IRAs. The collection of shares an individual has in different companies is called his or her portfolio.

stores. Workers laid more phone wires to accommodate the rising demand for home phones. Phone wires eventually stretched from one end of the country to the other. Telephone company stocks rose, and investors saw the industry as a worthy investment.

But what happened once everyone finally had a phone installed in his or her home? The telephone bubble did not burst. Technology kept improving, and people would eventually replace their old and outdated phones with new and better ones. The price of phones even dropped because so many people demanded them. They became so affordable that people eventually began to buy more than one phone for their homes. Then cell phones were introduced in the late-twentieth century, entirely reinvigorating the industry and stoking renewed consumer enthusiasm.

Bull and Bear Markets

Experienced investors know that the stock market will always go through periods of prosperity and periods of slow growth (or even zero or negative growth). The term used to describe a period of faster growth and prosperity is "bull market." Like a bull, the market charges on, strong and fierce. During a bull market, stock prices rise and investors make a lot of money. Soon more and more investors see their colleagues making money and decide they want in on the action, too. So they pour more and more money into the stock market, hoping for similarly big returns on their investment.

A period of economic slowdown is called a bear market. It is thought that the term dates back to the time when traders sold valuable bearskins. These skins were sold during periods in which traders feared that the prices of goods were falling. They wanted to get as much money for the bearskins as possible while they still could, so they sold

This sculpture of a bull stands in a plaza near Wall Street and the New York Stock Exchange in lower Manhattan. A bull market is one in which stocks are soaring.

at a reduced price. Another explanation for the term is that a bear tears its prey with its claws in a downward motion. A bull, on the other hand, goes after its opponent by pushing upward with its horns.

A bull market and a bear market are opposites of each other. The market normally moves slowly from one kind to another. Investors make more money during a bull market, and it is a symbol of a strong economy. In fact, there is a giant bronze statue of a bull prominently situated in the middle of Wall Street, very close to the NYSE.

Ending a Recession

How do recessions end? Money has to be injected back into the cash-starved economy through private investments, public spending, and greater access to loans and credit. Presidents who lead during a recession often try to do something to help the economy get back on its feet and start producing again. In an attempt to end the devastating and traumatic Great Depression,

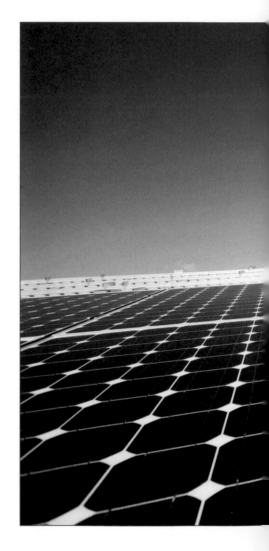

U.S. president Franklin Delano Roosevelt introduced the New Deal in the 1930s. The New Deal gave money to people who needed loans. It also introduced massive public spending and construction projects, such as the building of roads, bridges,

To end a recession, new job markets and opportunities are often needed to attract workers. Investment in new industries and technologies, like green energy, can stimulate a stalled economy.

and buildings. The project put many people back to work and eventually brought money back into the economy.

Another way to end a recession, inject cash back into a stalled economy, and stimulate upward movement in the stock market is for the government to give its citizens money to spend as they wish. During the presidency of George W. Bush, citizens received tax rebate checks that they could spend in any way they saw fit. The hope was that they would use the money to buy goods or services, putting money back into a weakening economy and stimulating it into solid growth and expansion.

During the presidency of Barack Obama, government money was given to various private organizations and state governments. This was done in order to create more jobs and prevent the country from sliding into an even deeper recession. Similar to the concept—if not the massive size—of the New Deal, President Obama's stimulus plan focused on providing jobs that might help improve the nation's roads, bridges, and buildings. It also focused on increasing green technologies. These are technologies that would help reduce our dependence on nonrenewable and environmentally harmful resources, such as fossil fuels.

Investing in Good Times and Bad

Investing in the stock market can be a risky business. In a way, it is a game of chance because the investor does not know how the company or the economy will perform over time. Some of the most successful shareholders think about how their investments will perform over the long run instead of focusing

People who are closer to retirement should take fewer risks in the stock market. Safer investments in reliable companies and industries will help protect their savings.

on short-term gains ("making a quick buck"). Retirement investments are often viewed this same way. In fact, the age of the investor and his or her likely retirement date is considered when 401(k) plans and IRAs are invested. Because the market has natural swings of up and down times, a young investor is encouraged to take greater risks in his or her stock choices. This will give the person a greater chance for sudden gains in profit. Investment risks (in new companies or technologies, for example) can be taken in hopes for great gains. If there are losses, the person will still have many years before retirement to make up the lost money.

As investors get older and closer to retirement, they are often advised to sell their riskier stocks and buy ones in more stable, well-established companies. Although the stock prices may not rise quickly like those of a new and untested company might, the investments are in companies that have a proven track record of consistent gains. The thought is, that during a slower economic time, less risky, blue chip stocks will perform more consistently than the riskier stocks of new or unproven companies. There is no guarantee that stocks will make money for the stockholder. It is even possible that older investors may lose their money—their retirement "nest egg"—right before they planned to retire and live off of it. This will mean they will have to continue working—or go back to work—at an advanced age, when they had been hoping to slow down. The security and leisure time that they had hoped to enjoy after decades of hard work and worry are suddenly taken away from them.

CHAPTER THREE
The Payoffs and Perils of Investing

When a company is successful and makes profits, it can sometimes offer some of those profits to its shareholders. This makes the idea of buying that company's stock even more attractive to investors. The money a company gives its shareholders on a regular basis is called a dividend. Dividends are usually given out each quarter year. And a small amount, usually less than a dollar, is given for each share that a stockholder owns. For example, if a shareholder owns one thousand shares of a company and the company offers a forty-cent dividend for each share, the stockholder will receive $400 each quarter.

Dividend amounts may be increased or decreased based on the company's performance, or the company may decide not to give dividends at all. During bull markets, investors who hold shares in strongly performing companies stand to make a lot of money in dividends. This is another reason why stockholders often hold onto their shares in a company instead of constantly selling them at the first sign of a decrease in profits.

Stock Splits

Sometimes stock prices may rise too high for many people to be able to afford them. Other times a company's stock prices

American radio executive Mel Karmazin announced that $530 million in investment money had been raised to help support the struggling satellite radio company Sirius XM.

will rise much higher than those of its competitors, making it less attractive to new investors. In response, the company's board of directors may decide to split the number of shares available for purchase. This usually means that, for every one

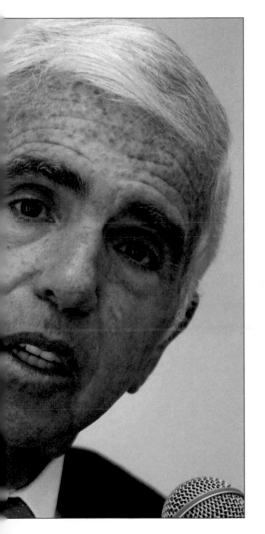

share of stock owned, the stockholder will now have two shares of stock. The value of each share will be cut in half. This makes the price of stocks half as much as they were before, so new investors may be interested in buying into the company. They have proof that the company is successful because it just split its stock, a sure sign of strong stock market performance. And the prices have been sharply reduced per share, making investment in the high-performing company far more affordable.

Shareholders who have gone through a stock split will now have twice the number of shares they once held in the company, but the overall value of their stock will remain the same. So instead of owning one share at $10, they now own two shares at $5 each. The overall value of their stock is the same as before.

So what is the benefit of a stock split besides attracting new investors? Ultimately, the company's long-term investors will also benefit from a stock split. A new, lower price will make the stock more attractive to new investors. When they buy into the stock, the prices will be driven up. For example, if the new $5 stock goes up another dollar, the original shareholders will then have two shares at $6 each. So without investing any new money, the original shareholder now has $12 instead of $10. This rise in the stock's price may not have occurred if not for the influx of new investors. If an investor remains a shareholder for a long time, he or she may experience several splits of a stock, and his or her number of shares will keep doubling and increasing.

A Stock Market Giant

We can see real-life examples of how the stock market works by examining the fortunes of a few companies throughout their history. One stock market success story can be found in the oil industry. Back in the 1860s, John D. Rockefeller made a fortune building processing plants that refined petroleum. He recognized and anticipated the public demand for oil. The machines of the Industrial Revolution required oil to keep them working. People also used oil in kerosene lamps in their homes. In 1870, Rockefeller formed the Standard Oil Company, which included his refining plants. The supply of oil was great at this time, and new sources of it were being found all the time. By 1879, the Standard Oil Company controlled 90 percent of the oil market.

In the years to come, Standard Oil grew and changed many times. The company bought more and more oil fields.

John D. Rockefeller's company Standard Oil controlled most of the oil industry in the late 1800s.

As far back as 1877, Standard Oil purchased another company, Vacuum Oil Company, that it thought would help it continue to grow and produce new products. The act of purchasing or obtaining another company is known as acquisition. Companies continue to do this today as a means of growing their business. It helps them expand their offerings, gain an edge over competitors, and offer their shareholders a way to make even more money.

Standard Oil continued to grow during the twentieth century, thanks in large part to the development of fuel-burning cars, trucks, buses, and airplanes. People suddenly needed oil, refined into gasoline, to transport themselves from place to place. There was a great demand for this resource, and shareholders made more and more money as the years went by. The company reacted to the ups and downs of the economy throughout the twentieth century. But it was successful enough to offer shareholders regular dividends and several stock splits.

Dot-com Investments

Not every public company is a stock market success story. While the oil industry became another "gold rush" in the late 1800s, so, too, did the dot-com industry in the 1990s. In the early part of the decade, the Internet was still a new, mostly unexplored world for the American public. Suddenly everyone was talking about cyberspace, the World Wide Web, and the information superhighway. It was predicted that everyone would soon have his or her own personal computer and that people would talk to each other via electronic mail and instant

Getting in on the Ground Floor

Before investing in the stock market, many investors do some research. They want to be reasonably sure that their stock will do well. So they must consider the product they are buying, the state of the industry the company is in, and the current economic times. For example, when the radio was first invented, investors bought shares of companies that manufactured radios, supplied radio parts, and produced and broadcast radio programs. But then times changed, and entertainment industry technology evolved. When television came along, there were fewer investors in radio. Investment dollars began to flow to television and its related fields.

Today, newer fields, especially green industries and computer, Internet, and information technologies, are the cutting-edge or "emerging" areas. These are areas in which investors may be able to make a large return on a relatively modest investment. The trick is to invest in smaller companies about to release an innovative breakthrough product or patent a revolutionary technology that will become the "next big thing." Once this new product or technology hits the market and generates buzz, excitement, and demand, the company's stock price will rise quickly. The stock of a start-up company may be worth $1 a share, but rise to $100 share soon after a major product release. An investor who gets in early by buying ten thousand shares for $10,000 would find the same ten thousand shares suddenly worth $1 million. If the investor sold his or her shares at this point, he or she would make a $990,000 profit. That is the ultimate good return on an investment!

messaging. They would shop in virtual malls without having to leave their houses. And they could seek and find any information they needed in what amounted to the largest resource library ever to exist in human history. Needless to say, there was also a lot of money to be made in this wild frontier of a brave new cyberworld.

Start-up companies sprang up everywhere to meet this new and sudden demand for content on the Internet. Even though the information technology (IT) industry was just getting started, investors eagerly snatched up the stock of IT start-up companies. They did so even when these companies had yet to produce and market an actual product or service. Web companies with Web addresses that ended in ".com" (short for "commerce") became the recipients of millions of dollars of investors' money. Some of these companies offered little more than a ".com" in their name. They often had no business plan, no product, and no income other than investor money.

Nevertheless, these companies felt confident that they

had something to offer the public. Investors gave them millions of dollars for their initial public offering, or IPO. That means investors gave the company enough money to issue stock to the public at a certain price. A dot-com bubble

WorldCom was a telecommunications giant whose stock soared in the late 1990s, but began to slip by the turn of the twenty-first century. The company declared bankruptcy in 2002.

occurred because people invested an incredible amount of money, often in companies that had nothing tangible to offer or sell, even after several years of investment. Stock prices were higher than they should have been. Their prices were far higher than the actual companies, their products, and their potential were worth.

Just because a company has a good idea doesn't mean that the idea will succeed. Plenty of entrepreneurs put their ideas to work during the dot-com bubble of the late 1990s. However, by around 2001, many of them had failed and went out of business. Their investors lost thousands, and sometimes millions, of dollars.

The dot-com bubble burst between 2000 and 2001. Countless start-ups had hopes of becoming the next huge company offering people popular goods and services on the Internet. When these dreams did not come true, thousands of workers were laid off. Wall Street suffered from plummeting stock prices. Investors lost millions. And the country sunk into a recession, which had an impact on the larger economy, even affecting people who did not work or invest in the IT industry.

Not every dot-com was a bust, however. Some of the companies that we now rely on and use every day to make our

Not all dot-coms were a bust. Some ideas that came out of the early days of the Internet have become things we rely on every day, such as deliveries from Amazon.com.

lives easier got their start during the era of the dot-com bubble. Google, Amazon, and eBay are all dot-com success stories. Google has changed the way people research on the Internet, and it has introduced the concept of free information with its programs Google Earth and Google Street View. Amazon and eBay have changed the way people search and shop for products. They have established new virtual markets for buying and selling. And they have found innovative ways to match sellers with buyers, allowing consumers to find even the most rare items for sale at competitive prices.

CHAPTER FOUR

The Stock Market Crash and the Great Depression

Sometimes we wonder how the stock market affects our everyday lives. For those who are not investors or who do not work for a publicly traded company, the connection may be more difficult to see. But the best example of how the stock market ultimately affects everyone is provided by the Great Depression in the United States during the 1930s.

The Roaring Twenties

To fully understand that period, it helps to look at the years that came before the biggest economic downturn in U.S. history. The 1920s were a time of great prosperity in the United States. World War I was over. There were many new inventions and technologies offering an easier life for people, including cars, refrigerators, gas stoves, telephones, radios, and even movies.

It was a time when many large companies rose and became popular with the public. The electric companies General Electric and Westinghouse, the Radio Corporation of America (RCA),

The Roaring Twenties were known as a time of great excess, high living, free spending, and carefree financial prosperity.

and many others proved that they could make a lot of money for their investors. They inspired such confidence that more ordinary people, rather than high finance types, felt emboldened to invest their money in these corporations. For the first time,

NO SMOKING

investing in the stock market became more commonplace for the average American.

The era became known as the Roaring Twenties. The stock market became a game for many Americans. People who did not even have the cash to buy stocks could still borrow money from the bank, invest, wait for their stock prices to rise, and then use some of their profits to pay back the bank loan.

This was an unusual economic time. Stock prices kept rising and rising because more and more people were investing in companies. Many newer and first-time investors did not know much about the companies they were investing in. They merely made guesses about the companies based on their names or what they thought the company produced. Everyone expected to make a profit overnight. Some stocks rose from $20 to $300 a share in just a matter of months. At this time, the average investor did not think about the risks of the stock market. There was a growing belief that the market would rise indefinitely, that there was no upper limit.

The Stock Market Crashes

As the 1920s came to an end, so did the "roaring" and prosperous days of the stock market. In September 1929, stock prices began to slip. But just as soon as they fell, the prices seemed to recover themselves. Sometimes investors ended up with even more money than before after these upward surges. But as October came, dips in the market became more common, and the market seemed less of a sure thing. Investors became a bit more nervous about the economy and less willing to pour money into stocks. People were no longer confident that their stocks were going to be a sure-fire way to keep making money. As people sold off their stocks and stopped investing in new ones, stock prices slipped further.

Then on Wednesday, October 23, a sudden and large rush of investors wanted to sell their stocks, all in the last hour of trading. It was a lightning-fast shock to the market. Some stock prices dropped more than $10

in that final hour, and more than two-and-a-half million shares were traded during that short time. As the closing bell rang, investors were panicked. The stock market was beginning to crash.

Following the news of the stock market crash of October 1929, crowds of people flocked to Wall Street to try to find out more.

The next day, Thursday, October 24, the panic continued. A huge stock market crash was underway, driven largely by people's fears. Fear and panic can cause investors to pull their money out of an investment quickly and cause prices to plummet. As the New York Stock Exchange opened that morning, investors began selling immediately. There seemed to be no one willing to buy up these shares. Everyone suddenly had the same goal—dumping their stocks for any price they could. People crowded the streets in panic. By the end of the day, the total value of dumped stocks was $14 billion. That's a lot of money, even by today's standards. However, back in 1929, the figure was unbelievably large. The entire annual budget of the U.S. government at the time was only $3 billion. Nearly five times the annual budget of the country was lost in just one day of trading.

The panic on Wall Street did not stop there. Over the next few days of trading, more and more investors sold off their stocks for increasingly low prices. "Black Tuesday," October 29, was the darkest day on Wall Street. More than $8 billion more in stock values had disappeared. From Wednesday, October 23, to Tuesday, October 29, the stock market lost more than $25 billion. Brokers were exhausted, some not having been home for

Bank collapses wiped out the savings of many people. This New York bank was shut down before its depositors could withdraw their money.

days because of the huge amount of paperwork that had to be filled out and filed due to the high volume of trading.

As word spread of the stock market crash and people had less hope for its quick recovery, insecurity about money spread from the stock market to the banking industry. Banks had lent out a lot of money to stock market investors. The hope was that the investor could make money in stocks and then pay back the bank with interest. (Interest is a sort of fee charged for borrowing money.)

After the stock market collapsed, many banks were left with no money on hand. Most of it was loaned out, and there was no chance the borrowers would be able to repay it. Depositors rushed to their banks to withdraw their money, fearing that the banks would fail due to these bad loans. The banks did not have enough to hand out to everyone who wished to withdraw their money. Today, there are laws to prevent this from happening. But back then, people lost their savings because they were left in banks that had made reckless loans. Not everyone who lost everything was a stock market investor.

A Decade-Long Depression

The crash of 1929 was too much for the market to bounce back from. This was much more than just a brief slump in stocks. Some people who had invested their entire life savings in the stock market had lost everything during the crash. Many people not only dumped their stocks at bargain-basement prices or held them and watched their value plummet. Sometimes they also lost the money they needed to pay back the banks that helped them buy those stocks in the first place.

That money had been tied up in the stock market, and it disappeared when the stock market crashed. As a result, banks failed because they could not cover the cost of those loans that would now never be repaid.

Many people had to sell all their possessions in order to raise enough money for basic necessities like clothes, food, and shelter. People sold their cars, houses, jewelry, and anything else they could get money for. Given the widespread economic collapse and suffering, though, they usually received rock-bottom prices for these valuables.

The full effects of the stock market crash would not be felt, however, for months and even years. Companies that saw their stocks plummet had little money left to operate, produce goods, or pay employees. Unemployment rose as companies went through difficult times and laid off workers. So people who did not even have their money invested in the stock market were affected by the crash.

The country sank deeper and deeper into an economic slowdown. By 1933, one out of every four Americans was out of work. People could not meet their mortgage payments, and they lost their homes and farms. Families suffering from unemployment could not spend on consumer goods or entertainment. This caused other businesses, such as restaurants and stores, to go out of business. As a result, even more workers were laid off. Once-wealthy businessmen were forced to sell fruit on street corners in order to make enough money to eat. People set up wooden or cardboard shelters in city parks. These shantytowns became known as "Hoovervilles." They were named after Herbert Hoover, who was president of the United States at the time of the crash. Hoover was roundly criticized for doing

The Great Depression lasted nearly a decade and left many formerly well-to-do people penniless, homeless, and unemployed.

nothing to stimulate the failing economy or alleviate the suffering of millions of impoverished, hungry, unemployed, and desperate Americans.

Recovery: The New Deal and World War II

With every economic downturn comes an eventual upturn and return to prosperity. The entire decade of the 1930s was difficult for Americans. President Roosevelt tried to fix the economy with a massive economic stimulus plan. Americans were suffering so much from the Great Depression that he promised "a new deal for the American people."

The New Deal put people back to work building bridges, roads, schools, libraries, public office buildings, and other important and useful structures. This provided the families of these workers with money for life's basic necessities, like food, clothing, and shelter. In addition, the program helped improve the nation's transportation infrastructure at a time when more good, paved roads and safe and convenient bridges were desperately needed.

An important part of Roosevelt's response to the stock market crash, its causes, and the resulting Great Depression was the creation of the Securities and Exchange Commission (SEC). The SEC protects investors by monitoring and regulating the sale of stocks in the stock market. It oversees the work of stockbrokers to make sure that they are carrying out the wishes of their clients. The Federal Deposit Insurance Corporation, or FDIC, another Roosevelt creation, also protects the American people from losing money. The FDIC insures the money that people deposit into their checking and savings accounts. The government guarantees that it will cover

World War II helped create many jobs in America, especially for women who had to go to work in factories while men fought in the war.

the amount of money owed to depositors if the bank does not have the money to do so.

There was a lot of help from the government to fight the Great Depression, get Americans working and spending again, and ensure that what caused the crash would not happen again. Yet prosperity did not return to the United States until about ten years after the crash of the stock market. It was not until after America entered into World War II that the Great Depression ended.

At this time, thousands of Americans were needed to make goods for the war, such as tanks, planes, jeeps, battleships, artillery, armor, ammunition, and uniforms. Factories opened and wartime materials were produced in massive volume. Huge legions of workers—mainly women, since the young men were off fighting the war—were put to work in factories and even on the stock market trading floor. Stocks in companies that produced goods for the war effort became stable and strong again.

By the time the war ended, the country had recovered from the Great Depression. In fact, the United States had become the richest country in the world. It was now one of only two military superpowers, along with the Soviet Union, a wartime ally and postwar rival.

MYTHS and FACTS

MYTH   No one saw the stock market crash of 1929 coming.

FACT   There were a few people who predicted that stock prices could not continue to stay as high as they were. Some investors observed the dwindling money supply in banks, the huge amount of cash lent out to investors, and the highly inflated prices of stocks and knew that a problem was bound to arise. They correctly saw that a slump in stock prices would result in widespread defaults on these loans and a cash crisis for the banks, which would not be able to cover the deposits of their ordinary customers.

MYTH   Everyone thought the New Deal was a good idea and a great success.

FACT   There were critics of President Roosevelt who believed that the government should not take such a strong and active role in managing the economy. They believed that rules and regulations kept businesses from doing what they wanted to grow, expand, and make money.

MYTH   The stock market crash was the cause of the Great Depression.

FACT   Many economists believe that the country was already entering a recession at the time the stock market crashed. The period of prosperity had allowed many Americans to buy goods such as cars, homes, telephones, and radios. Yet having acquired these consumer goods, the demand for the products had begun to decrease during the late 1920s. Unemployment had already been rising before the stock market crash. So it may have been the weakening economy that actually prompted the stock market crash.

CHAPTER FIVE

The Stock Market Today

S tarting in 2007, the United States entered another difficult period of economic downturn. Economists have
compared this severe recession to the Great Depression and
the period of time before and after the stock market crash
of 1929. While the recession of the late 2000s was not as
catastrophic as the Great Depression, there are several simi-
larities that can help people better understand the problems
the country faced.

The Real Estate Bubble

During the late 1990s and first half of the 2000s, there was a
financial boom in the real estate industry. It became easier
and easier for people to get a mortgage (a loan to help buy a
home). Normally, a mortgage is based on the income of the
potential buyer, as well as the person's ability to repay the loan
and his or her credit history (the person's track record of pay-
ing bills and repaying loans). Banks became more lenient and

lent money to people who could not really afford the houses they bought. They didn't have enough income, and often they had poor credit histories. What's worse, banks lent them money in a way that would cause their payments to go up

The real estate market was one of the major causes of the recession that began in 2007. Poor lending practices, inflated prices, and homeowner defaults led to a burst housing bubble.

dramatically—and sometimes unexpectedly for those home-owners who didn't read the fine print—after a few months of relatively low mortgage payments. This often put the monthly house payments beyond the range of the new homeowners.

This poor lending practice is sometimes referred to as "predatory lending." It was ignored by bank regulating authorities, mainly because home prices kept rising along with demand, and banks kept making more and more profits. No one wanted to stem this rising tide of seeming prosperity.

Construction workers enjoyed the boom in new home building. Banks enjoyed the flood of new customers. The stock market enjoyed the rising profits and stock prices of banks, mortgage lenders, and other financial institutions. All of this freewheeling lending and spending and building and buying occurred in part because the government's central bank, the Federal Reserve, was being especially hands-off. It was not carefully monitoring or regulating the business practices of many lenders and other financial institutions.

Collapse, Defaults, and Foreclosures

Buyers in over their heads, reckless lenders, and a lax and inattentive federal government all played a role in creating the

Irresponsible lending by banks caused many homeowners to lose their homes when they could not afford the skyrocketing mortgages. This had a negative ripple effect on the entire economy.

housing bubble and the economic crisis that followed its bursting. In late 2008, a stock market crash alerted the country to the trouble that had been brewing for more than a year. Starting on October 6, 2008, the stock market slipped into an eight-day

slide and collapse of stock prices. During that same period, the Dow Jones Industrial Average lost 22 percent of its value, or about 2,400 points. The market was very shaky for a period after that, sometimes gaining a little bit of value back, only to lose even more over the next couple of days.

At the same time that stocks were tanking, many people who were given subprime mortgages were defaulting on their payments, and banks were foreclosing on their homes. This meant the people had to move out of their homes, which would be seized and sold off by the banks that had issued their mortgages. The banks now owned the homes, so they kept any money raised by their sale. Nevertheless, because they had made so many reckless loans that would not be repaid, the banks could no longer cover all the deposits made by their checking and savings account customers. Banks began to fail, and mortgage companies entered a crisis. In some cases, the government had to step in and use money from the Federal Reserve to cover bank losses. Billions of dollars were lost by these banks and mortgage companies about a month before the stock market crashed.

Ripple Effects

Meanwhile, more and more people lost their homes. Bank failures left banks unable to lend money to average citizens and companies that needed loans. Consumers stopped spending. Companies were forced to lay off workers. Less money went into the economy. The cycle of economic decline sped up quickly.

By 2009, most Americans were affected in some manner. Problems now existed in sectors other than the mortgage and banking industries. Unemployment rose to nearly 10 percent around the country. Although it was not as severe as the downturn of the 1930s, the financial crisis facing the country was similar to the one that occurred during the Great Depression.

With a poor economy comes hard times. Small businesses failed because they could not get loans from banks to continue their operations. Larger companies and state and federal governments were forced to cut their budgets to make up for lost revenue.

The financial difficulties of the United States also affected the rest of the world because the United States does so much business with companies around the globe. Cutbacks in production and reduced overseas demand for U.S. products translated

The recession of 2008–2009 affected many large corporations and banks. Circuit City, a giant electronics retailer, is one of the many companies that went out of business during the recession.

into fewer exports. The collapse in American consumer spending translated into fewer imports. As a result, both American and international companies experienced a sales slump and laid off workers, further reducing consumer spending. Economies around the world suffered. So did the stock prices of U.S. and foreign companies. The recession that began with the burst bubble in the American housing industry had gone global.

The Federal Government to the Rescue?

Just as the United States slid into a financial crisis, Americans were choosing a new commander in chief. The new president, Barack Obama, was faced with the tough decision of how to fix the economy. Should the federal government stay out of economic policy, as some economists suggest, and let market forces correct the problems? Or should the government attempt to reverse the economic freefall and protect its citizens from the harshest effects of the recession?

Part of the reason why people voted for Barack Obama was because he had expressed a strong determination to be active and aggressive in his attempts to revive the economy. On January 28, 2009, the House of Representatives approved an $819 billion economic recovery plan. It would take time for the money to be fully distributed. It would take even longer to tell if the spending plan worked and helped reverse the recession.

There will always be ups and downs in the stock market. There will be winners and losers. The same people who are winners one day can become losers the next day. People who once thought they lost it all in the stock market can suddenly find that they have made a fortune. The same risk that drives some people away from this kind of money investment can attract others.

The stock market is not always a hair-raising roller-coaster ride, characterized by dramatic peaks and stomach-churning drops. The general trend of the stock market over the last two hundred years and more has been a solid and steady upward swing, with occasional—and occasionally steep—setbacks. Over time, most investors see a healthy return on their investments, usually far outstripping the interest that money can earn in a savings account. Investors must be aware of the risks, research their investments, invest only a portion of their savings, and spread their money around to many different companies to minimize the chance of sudden huge losses. If they do these things, investing in the stock market can be a fairly reliable and effective way to increase personal wealth, support American corporations, and keep the economy humming.

Ten Great Questions
to Ask a Financial Adviser

1 What can a financial adviser do for me and my savings?

2 Should I invest my money myself, or should I use a financial adviser?

3 My parents have an account called a 529 to help pay for my college tuition. What is this?

4 How much of my savings should I invest in the stock market?

5 When I research a company before buying stock, what should I try to find out about the company?

6 Should I sell my stock during a recession, or downturn, in the economy?

7 Should I take advice from other people who tell me what kind of stocks to buy?

8 Should I check the price of my stock every day?

9 Is it better to buy stocks in companies that are brand new or that have been around for a long time?

10 What should I do with the profits I make from the stock market?

GLOSSARY

acquisition The act of buying or obtaining something.

bear market A period of falling stock prices.

bull market A period of rising stock prices.

capitalism An economic system in which trade and industry can be privately owned, rather than government-owned, and designed to make a profit for the owners.

commodity A good that is sold before being processed, such as wheat, tobacco, or cotton.

depression A period of prolonged and deep economic recession.

dividend The amount of money paid by companies to their shareholders.

economy The growth or wealth of a region or country.

Federal Reserve The system of federal banks that controls the U.S. money supply.

foreclose To take away a person's property because of failure to keep up with mortgage payments.

initial public offering (IPO) The first time a company sells shares of its ownership—stocks—to the public.

investor A person who spends money on a company or enterprise and expects to make a profit in return.

merger The combination of two or more entities, such as companies, into one.

prosperity A period of economic success, growth, and wealth.

public company A company that sells shares of its ownership to the public.

recession A period of economic decline.

regulation The rules made and enforced by a governing authority.

securities Certificates of stocks that prove a person's partial ownership of a company.

share A unit of ownership in a company; a share of stock.

split The breaking up or dividing of stocks in order to lower per share prices.

start-up company A newly created company with no previous business history.

stock A unit of ownership in a company.

subprime mortgage A type of mortgage (loan to buy a house) given to people with low income and often poor credit ratings.

trading The buying and selling of stocks.

FOR MORE INFORMATION

American Association of Individual Investors
625 North Michigan Avenue
Chicago, IL 60611
(800) 428-2244
Web site: http://www.aaii.com
The AAII is a nonprofit organization that provides education
for individual investors so that they can effectively manage
their own stock portfolios.

Canadian Stock Exchange
First Canadian Place
77 Adelaide Street West
Toronto, ON M5X 1A4
Canada
(888) 873-8392
Web site: http://www.tsx.com
The Canadian Stock Exchange was established in 1852 and
continues to help companies become listed in a world
market. It also helps investors enter the world market.

Department of Finance Canada
140 O'Connor Street
19th Floor, East Tower
Ottawa, ON K1A 0G5

Canada
(613) 992-1573
Web site: http://www.fin.gc.ca
The Department of Finance Canada plans and prepares the
budget for the Canadian government. It also establishes
rules and regulations for Canadian banks and finance
institutions.

Investment Company Institute
National Association of U.S. Investment Companies
1401 H Street NW, Suite 1200
Washington, DC 20005
(202) 326-5800
Web site: http://www.ici.org
The Investment Company Institute is an association of U.S.
investment companies. Its Web site includes research,
statistics, and information about investments.

National Endowment for Financial Education
5299 DTC Boulevard, Suite 1300
Greenwood Village, CO 80111
(303) 741-6333
Web site: http://www.nefe.org
This organization is a private, nonprofit, national foundation
devoted to educating Americans about finance and improving their financial well-being. The organization includes an
educational program for high school students.

U.S. Securities and Exchange Commission
100 F Street NE

Washington, DC 20549
(202) 942-8088
Web site: http://www.sec.gov
The SEC oversees the activities of stock exchanges and stock-
    brokers. It aims to protect investors and keep the trading of
    stocks as fair and orderly as possible.

Web Sites

Due to the changing nature of Internet links, Rosen
Publishing has developed an online list of Web sites related to
the subject of this book. This site is updated regularly. Please
use this link to access the list:

http://www.rosenlinks.com/rwe/stoc

FOR FURTHER READING

Brezina, Corona. *How Deflation Works* (Real World Economics). New York, NY: Rosen Publishing Group, Inc., 2010.

Brezina, Corona. *How Stimulus Plans Work* (Real World Economics). New York, NY: Rosen Publishing Group, Inc., 2010.

Deatherage, Judi. *Who Wants to Be a Millionaire?* Lexington, KY: The Clark Group, 2007.

Fuller, Donna Jo. *The Stock Market*. Minneapolis, MN: Lerner Classroom, 2006.

Harman, Hollis Page. *Money Sense for Kids*. Hauppauge, NY: Barrons Educational Series, 2005.

Hart, Joyce. *How Inflation Works* (Real World Economics). New York, NY: Rosen Publishing Group, Inc., 2009.

Kelly, Jason. *The Neatest Little Guide to Stock Market Investing*. New York, NY: Penguin Group, 2009.

Lange, Brenda. *The Stock Market Crash of 1929: The End of Prosperity*. New York, NY: Facts on File, Inc. 2007.

Loewen, Nancy, and Brian Jensen. *Ups and Downs: A Book About the Stock Market*. Mankato, MN: Picture Window Books, 2005.

Minden, Celia. *Investing: Making Your Money Work for You*. Ann Arbor, MI: Cherry Lake Publishing, 2007.

Morrison, Jessica. *Investing*. New York, NY: Weigl
Publishers, Inc., 2009.

Nagle, Jeanne. *How a Recession Works* (Real World
Economics). New York, NY: Rosen Publishing
Group, Inc., 2009.

Orr, Tamra. *A Kid's Guide to Stock Market Investing*.
Hockessin, DE: Mitchell Lane Publishers, 2008.

Porterfield, Jason. *How a Depression Works* (Real World
Economics). New York, NY: Rosen Publishing Group,
Inc., 2009.

Roman, Rick. *I'm a $hareholder Kit: The Basics About
Stocks for Kids/Teens*. Portland, OR: Leading Edge
Gifts, 2009.

Western, David. *Booms, Bubbles, and Busts in the U.S. Stock
Market*. Oxford, England: Taylor & Francis, Inc., 2004.

BIBLIOGRAPHY

Blumenthal, Karen. *Six Days in October: The Stock Market Crash of 1929.* New York, NY: Atheneum Books for Young Readers, 2002.

Calmes, Jackie. "House Passes Stimulus Plan with No GOP Votes." *New York Times,* January 28, 2009. Retrieved September 2009 (http://www.nytimes.com/2009/01/29/us/politics/29obama.html).

Fraser, Steve. *Wall Street: America's Dream Palace.* New Haven, CT: Yale University Press, 2008.

German, Kent. "Top 10 Dot-com Flops." CNet. Retrieved June 2009 (http://www.cnet.com/1990-11136_1-6278387-1.html).

Kent, Zachary. *The Story of the New York Stock Exchange* (Cornerstones of Freedom). Chicago, IL: Children's Press, 1990.

Money-zine.com. "Stock Market Crash of 2008." Retrieved June 2009 (http://www.money-zine.com/Investing/Stocks/Stock-Market-Crash-of-2008).

New York Times. "Economic Stimulus: Latest Developments." June 26, 2009. Retrieved July 2009 (http://topics.nytimes.com/topics/reference/timestopics/subjects/u/united_states_economy/economic_stimulus).

Peter, Ian. "History of the Internet: The Dot-com Bubble." NetHistory.com. Retrieved June 2009 (http://www.

nethistory.info/History%20of%20the%20Internet/
dotcom.html).

Practical Small Business Information. "What Caused the
2008 Recession?" Retrieved June 2009 (http://
practicalsmallbusiness.info/recession/what-caused-
the-2008-recession).

Schoen, John. "Is This Another Great Depression?" MSNBC,
January 21, 2009. Retrieved June 2009 (http://www.
newsvine.com/_news/2009/01/21/2340049-is-this-
another-great-depression).

SEC.gov. "The Investor's Advocate: How the SEC Protects
Investors, Maintains Market Integrity, and Facilitates
Capital Formation." Retrieved June 2009 (http://www.
sec.gov/about/whatwedo.shtml).

Smith, Aaron. "Madoff's Day of Reckoning." CNN.com, June
29, 2009. Retrieved June 2009 (http://money.cnn.com/
2009/06/26/news/economy/madoff_sentence/index.htm).

StreetAuthority.com. "Initial Public Offering (IPO)."
Retrieved June 2009 (http://www.streetauthority.com/
terms/i/ipo.asp).

Whitcrafe, Melissa. *Wall Street* (Cornerstones of Freedom).
Chicago, IL: Children's Press, 2003.

Wilson, Andrew B. "Five Myths About the Great
Depression." *Wall Street Journal*, November 4, 2008.
Retrieved June 2009 (http://online.wsj.com/article/
SB122576077569495545.html).

XTimeline.com. "History of ExxonMobil." Retrieved June
2009 (http://www.xtimeline.com/timeline/History-of-
Exxon-Mobil).

INDEX

About the Author

Kathy Furgang is a full-time writer and editor specializing in the educational market for elementary and middle school students and teachers. She has written books for Rosen Central and PowerKids Press for more than ten years, including several titles on economic subjects. Furgang lives in upstate New York with her husband and two sons.

Photo Credits

Cover (top) © www.istockphoto.com/Lilli Day; cover (bottom), p. 1 (right) © Stephen Ferry/Liaison/Getty Images; pp. 7, 34–35, 42–43 © AP Images; p. 9 © Shutterstock; pp. 10–11, 46–47 © The Granger Collection; pp. 14–15, 20–21, 22–23 © Joe Raedle/Getty Images; pp. 16–17 © Brad Barket/Getty Images; pp. 26–27 © Serge Attal/Time-Life Pictures/Getty Images; pp. 28–29 © Dreamlight/Getty Images; p. 31 © Jose Luis Pelaez/Getty Images; p. 37 © Time-Life Pictures/Mansell/Getty Images; pp. 40–41 © Heather Hall/AFP/Getty Images; pp. 48–49 © MPI/Getty Images; pp. 50–51 © FPG/Hulton Archive/Getty Images; p. 54 © Archive Holdings, Inc./Getty Images; p. 56 © H. Armstrong Roberts/Retrofile/Getty Images; pp. 60–61 © www.istockphoto.com/Ann Marie Kurtz; pp. 62–63 © David McNew/Getty Images; p. 65 © Robyn Beck/AFP/Getty Images.

Designer: Sam Zavieh; Photo Researcher: Marty Levick